# Scale Etudes

JAMES "RED" McLEOD        NORMAN STASKA

## Intonation Accuracy and Rhythmic Precision for Individuals, Small Ensembles or Large Instrumental Groups.

### *Instrumentation . . .*

Db Piccolo

C Flute (C Piccolo, Oboe, Violin)

Bb Clarinet

Bb Bass Clarinet (Bb Tenor Saxophone)

Eb Alto Saxophone (Eb Horn, Eb Clarinet)

Eb Baritone Saxophone (Eb Alto Clarinet)

Viola

F Horn

Cornet (Trumpet)

Baritone T. C.

Trombone (Baritone B. C., Cello, Bassoon)

Tuba (String Bass)

Percussion (Tympani, Bells)

Conductor

## SCHMITT, HALL & McCREARY

SCHBK 9623E

# Key of G (B♭ Concert)

**E♭ Alto Saxophone**
**E♭ Horn**
**E♭ Clarinet**

Combination: W – Ex. 1
X – Ex. 3
Y – Ex. 7
Z – Ex. 9

## Major Scale

Use various articulations

**1**

Also play as: 𝅗𝅥, ♩, ♪ & ♪

### SUGGESTED RHYTHM PATTERNS
(Apply to numbers 1 through 6)

(a) (b) (c) (d) (e) (f) (g) (h)

1 2 3 4   1 2 3 4   1 2 3 4   1 2 3 4   1 2 3 4   1 2 (3) 4   1 (2) 3 4   (1) 2 3 4

For Duet – use with No. 1

## Interval Studies

(Thirds)

**2**

For Duet or Trio – use with Nos. 1 or 2

(Fourths)

**3**

For Duet, Trio, etc. – use with Nos. 1, 2 or 3

(Fifths)

**4**

Can be used with Nos. 1 through 4

(Sixths)

**5**

Can be used with Nos. 1 through 5

(Thirds & Fifths)

**6**

## Scale Studies

Can be used with Nos. 1 through 6

**7**

Can be used with Nos. 1 through 6

**8**

9066-B-32

e - Harmonic Minor (g Concert)

**4**

Chromatic

Nos. 14 & 14a can be played as a Duet

**14** (Scale)

**14a** (Study)

Scale Rhythmic Study – Round

**15** Ⓐ

Ⓑ

Ⓒ

Melody Study – How Can I Leave Thee

Kücken

Andante (SOLO)

**16** (HARMONY)

*mf*

*cresc.*

*f*

*dim. e rit.*

Chorale Studies

Exercises 17 through 20 can be used with No. 1

**17** Legato

Eb Alto Saxophone
Eb Horn
Eb Clarinet

Chorale Studies (cont.)
Technical Study for No. 17

5

Eb Alto Saxophone
Eb Horn
Eb Clarinet

# Key of C (Eb Concert)

Combination: W - Ex. 22
X - Ex. 25
Y - Ex. 21
Z - Ex. 24

Eb Alto Saxophone
Eb Horn
Eb Clarinet

Can be used with Nos. 21 through 26

**27**

Can be used with Nos. 21 through 27

**28**

Can be used with Nos. 21 through 27

**29**

Can be used with Nos. 21, 22 or 24

**30**

Can be used with Nos. 21, 22, 24, 25, 27 or 30

**31**

Can be used with Nos. 21 through 28

**32**

8

Eb Alto Saxophone
Eb Horn
Eb Clarinet

## a - Harmonic Minor (c Concert)

## Chromatic

Nos. 34 & 34a can be played as a Duet

## Scale Rhythmic Study – Round

## Melody Study – Drink To Me Only With Thine Eyes

Moderato

English Air

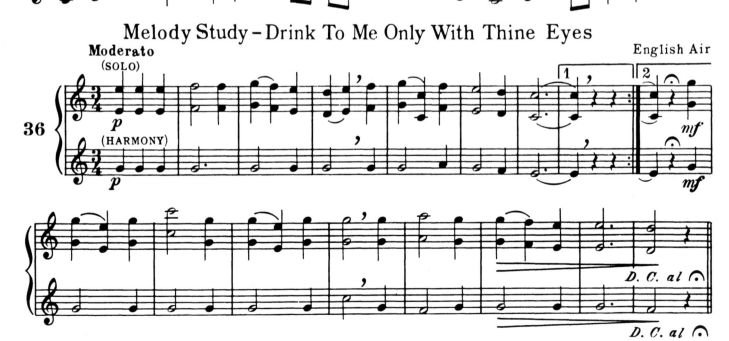

Exercises 37 through 40 can be used with No. 21

Technical Study for No. 38

Technical Study for No. 39

Eb Alto Saxophone
Eb Horn
Eb Clarinet

# Key of D (F Concert)

## Major Scale

Can be used with Nos. 41, 42 or 46

**49**

Can be used with Nos. 41, 42, 43, 46 or 47

**50**

Can be used with Nos. 41 through 44 or 46, 48 or 50

**51**

Can be used with Nos. 41 through 48 or 50

**52**

## b - Harmonic Minor (d Concert)

(Scale)

**53**

(Study)

**53 a**

# Chromatic

**E♭ Alto Saxophone**
**E♭ Horn**
**E♭ Clarinet**

Nos. 54 & 54a can be played as a Duet

## Scale Rhythmic Study – Round

## Melody Study – Anvil Chorus

Verdi

## Chorale Studies

Exercises 57 through 60a can be used with No. 41

Technical Study for No. 59

Technical Study for No. 60

# Key of F (A♭ Concert)

E♭ Alto Saxophone
E♭ Horn
E♭ Clarinet

## Major Scale

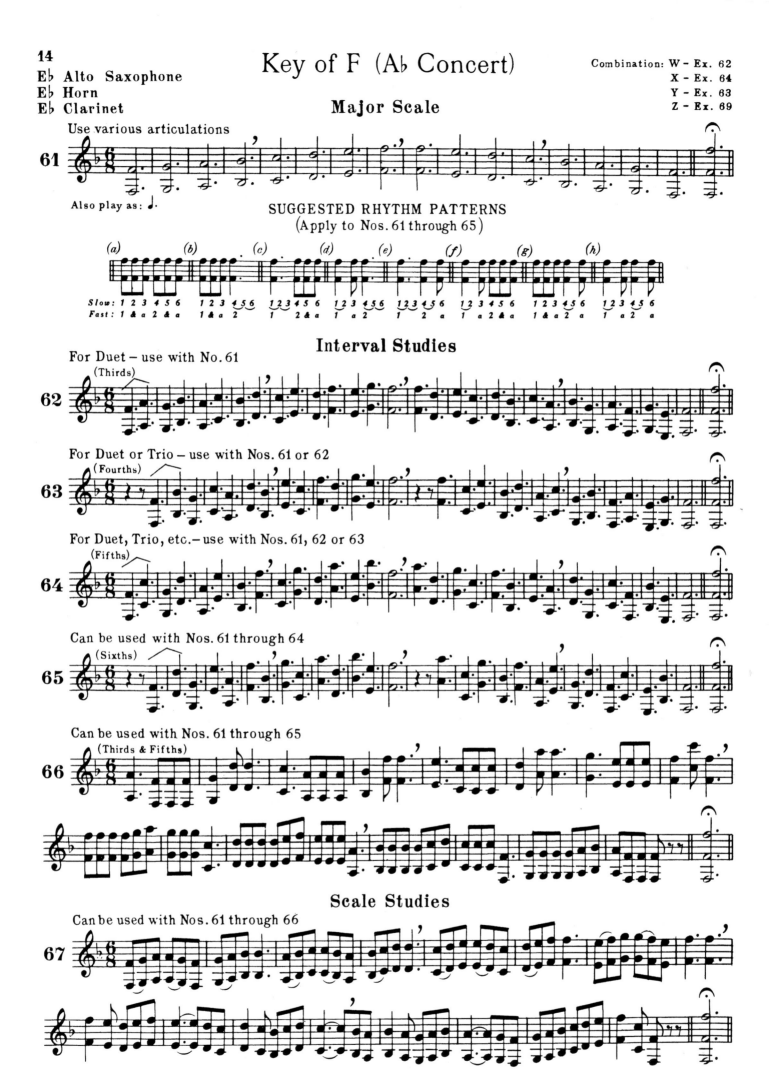

Use various articulations

**61**

Also play as: ♩.

### SUGGESTED RHYTHM PATTERNS
(Apply to Nos. 61 through 65)

## Interval Studies

For Duet – use with No. 61
(Thirds)
**62**

For Duet or Trio – use with Nos. 61 or 62
(Fourths)
**63**

For Duet, Trio, etc. – use with Nos. 61, 62 or 63
(Fifths)
**64**

Can be used with Nos. 61 through 64
(Sixths)
**65**

Can be used with Nos. 61 through 65
(Thirds & Fifths)
**66**

## Scale Studies

Can be used with Nos. 61 through 66
**67**

E♭ Alto Saxophone
E♭ Horn
E♭ Clarinet

Scale Studies (cont.)

15

Can be used with Nos. 61 through 64

Can be used with Nos. 61 through 66

Can be used with Nos. 61 through 67

Can be used with Nos. 61 through 66

Can be used with Nos. 61 through 67 & 70 or 71

**d - Harmonic Minor (f Concert)**

(Scale)

(Study)

9066 - B

Eb Alto Saxophone
Eb Horn
Eb Clarinet

# Chromatic

Nos. 74 & 74a can be played as a Duet

## Scale Rhythmic Study – Round

## Melody Study – Vive l'Amour

Moderato
(SOLO)

College Song

(HARMONY)

Exercises 77 through 80 can be used with No. 61

Technical Study for No.78

Technical Study for No.79

# Key of A (C Concert)

**E♭ Alto Saxophone**
**E♭ Horn**
**E♭ Clarinet**

Combination: W – Ex. 82
X – Ex. 86
Y – Ex. 87
Z – Ex. 83

## Major Scale

**Scale Studies**

20

Eb **Alto Saxophone**
Eb **Horn**
Eb **Clarinet**

## f♯ - Harmonic Minor (a Concert)

## Chromatic

Nos. 94 & 94a can be played as a Duet

## Scale Rhythmic Study–Round

## Melody Study – Julida Polka

9066-B

Eb Alto Saxophone
Eb Horn
Eb Clarinet

# Chorale Studies

Exercises 97 through 100a can be used with No. 81

**Technical Study for No. 99**

**Technical Study for No. 100**

9066-B

Eb Alto Saxophone
Eb Horn
Eb Clarinet

# Key of Bb (Db Concert)

## Major Scale

Use various articulations

Also play as:

### SUGGESTED RHYTHM PATTERNS
(Apply to the Scale)

## Interval Studies

For Duet – use with No. 101
(Thirds)

For Duet or Trio – use with Nos. 101 or 102
(Fourths)

For Duet, Trio, etc. – use with Nos. 101, 102 or 103
(Fifths)

Can be used with Nos. 101 through 104
(Thirds & Fifths)

## Scale Study

Can be used with Nos. 101 through 105

9066-B

**Chromatic Study**

**Melody Study – Juanita**

Andante Cantabile

Spanish Air

**Chorale Study**

This exercise can be used with No.101

Legato

Eb **Alto Saxophone**
Eb **Horn**
Eb **Clarinet**

# Key of E (G Concert)

Combination: W – Ex. 115
X – Ex. 116
Y – Ex. 114
Z – Ex. 112

## Major Scale

Use various articulations

**111**

Also play as: ♩, ♪, ♪ & ♪

## SUGGESTED RHYTHM PATTERNS
(Apply to Nos. 111 through 115)

*(a)*    *(b)*    *(c)*    *(d)*    *(e)*    *(f)*

1 & 2 & 3 4    1 2 3 & 4 &    1 & 2 & 3 &4 &    1 & 2 & 3 4 &    1 & a 2 3 4    1 2&a 3 4&a

## Interval Studies

For Duet – use with No. 111
(Thirds)

**112**

For Duet or Trio – use with Nos. 111 or 112
(Fourths)

**113**

For Duet, Trio, etc. – use with Nos. 111, 112 or 113
(Fifths)

**114**

Can be used with Nos. 111 through 114
(Octaves)

**115**

## Scale Study

Can be used with Nos. 111 through 115

**116**

Eb Alto Saxophone
Eb Horn
Eb Clarinet

**c♯ - Harmonic Minor (e Concert)**

(Scale)

**117**

(Study)

**117 a**

## Chromatic Study

**118**

## Melody Study – Coronation March

Meyerbeer

**Maestoso**
(SOLO)

**119**

(HARMONY)

## Chorale Study

This exercise can be used with No. 111

**Legato**

**120**

9066-B

Nos. 128 & 128a can be played as a Duet

**Melody Study – Celeste Aida**

Verdi

**Chorale Study**

This exercise can be used with No.121

Eb Alto Saxophone
Eb Horn
Eb Clarinet

# Key of B (D Concert)

Combination: W – Ex.132
X – Ex.133
Y – Ex.131
Z – Ex.134

## Major Scale

Use various articulations

**131**

Also play as: ♩, ♩, ♪ & ♪

### SUGGESTED RHYTHM PATTERNS
(Apply to Nos. 131 through 134)

(a)    (b)    (c)    (d)    (e)    (f)

## Interval Studies

For Duet – use with No. 131

**132** (Thirds)

For Duet or Trio – use with Nos. 131 or 132

**133** (Fourths)

For Duet, Trio, etc. – use with Nos. 131, 132 or 133

**134** (Fifths)

Can be used with Nos. 131 through 134

**135** (Thirds & Fifths)

## Scale Study

Can be used with Nos. 131 through 135

**136**

## g♯ - Harmonic Minor (b Concert)

**137** (Scale)

**137 a** (Study)

Nos. 138 & 138a can be played as a Duet

## Melody Study – Bluebells of Scotland

**Andante Moderato**

Scottish Folk Song

## Chorale Study

This exercise can be used with No. 131

**E♭ Alto Saxophone**
**E♭ Clarinet**

# High School Cadets

Sousa

March tempo

141

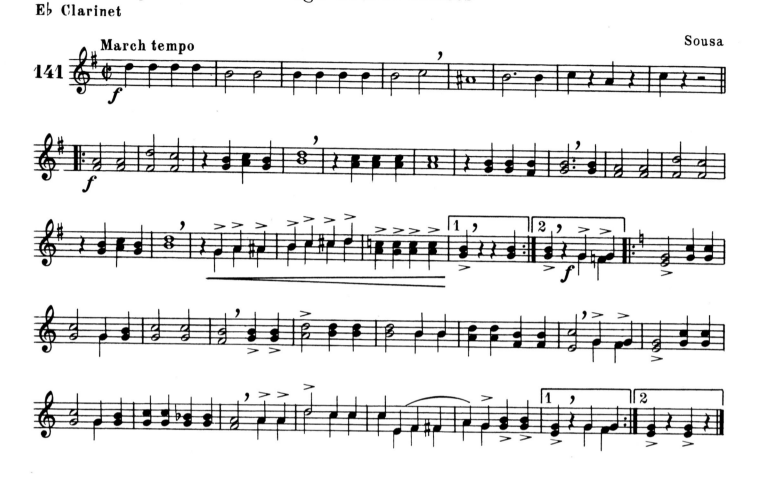

# High School Cadets

**E♭ Horn**

Sousa

March tempo

141
a

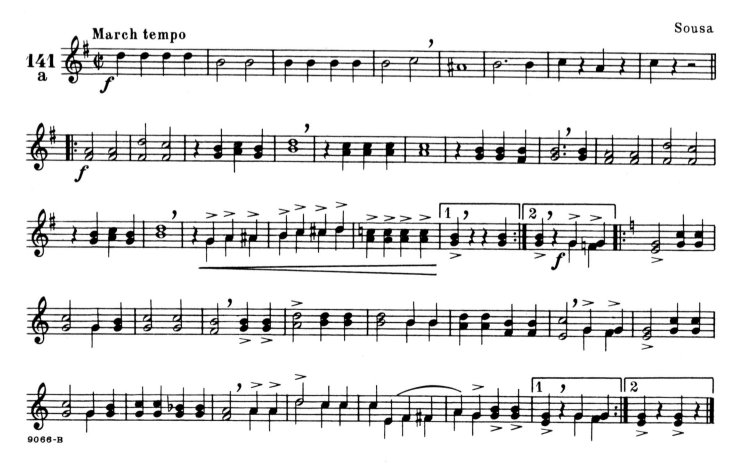

9066-B

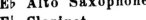

Eb Alto Saxophone
Eb Clarinet

# Grand March

Haydn

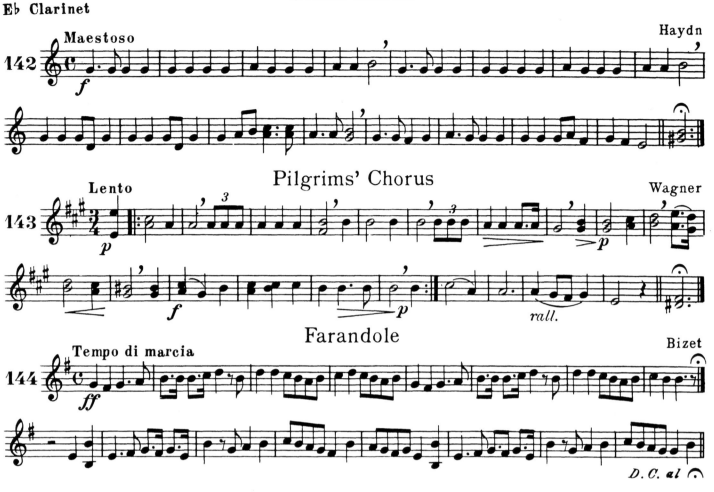

**142** Maestoso

## Pilgrims' Chorus

Wagner

**143** Lento

## Farandole

Bizet

**144** Tempo di marcia

D.C. al 𝄐

Eb Horn

# Grand March

Haydn

**142**
**a** Maestoso

## Pilgrims' Chorus

Wagner

**143**
**a** Lento

## Farandole

Bizet

**144**
**a** Tempo di marcia

9066-B

D.C. al 𝄐

Eb Alto Saxophone
Eb Clarinet

# Our Boys Will Shine Tonight

## Shoo Fly

## Guadeamus Igitur

Eb Horn

# Our Boys Will Shine Tonight

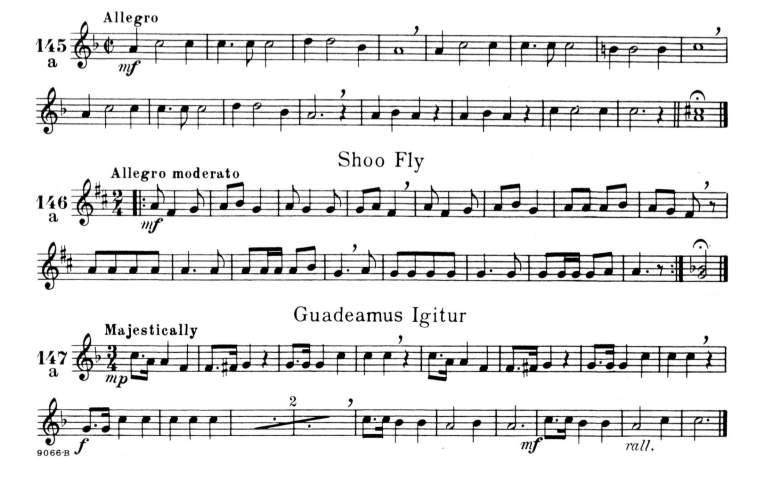

## Shoo Fly

## Guadeamus Igitur